BENEATH THE EMERALD MOON

THE WHISPERS OF A FERVENT HEART

Harine A.L

BookLeaf
Publishing

India | USA | UK

Made with ♥ on the BookLeaf Publishing Platform
www.bookleafpub.in
www.bookleafpub.com

Dedication

I dedicate this book to my parents, whom I'm blessed to have, for I shall be forever in debt for the love and affection I've been showered upon.

Preface

Poems, the embodiment of one's emotions and imagination, seep deep into the strings of reality whose rhythm is a play of the divinity.
Being of ethereal origin, I welcome the readers on this journey of having to experience the elegance and beauty of love.

Acknowledgements

Poems are what I call a window to the musings of one's soul, untouched yet truly felt in its entirety. A universe that is genuinely designed to allow one to experience the possibilities, those that are usually constrained by pragmatism.

I express my deepest gratitude to the almighty for giving me the strength and knowledge to write this book, while also thanking my very pillars of love and support—my family and friends—for their everlasting encouragement.

1. THE CELESTIAL BIRTH-GIVER

Shan't thy be a sinner's salvation,
An embodiment of the light in creation?
Enrapture shan't thy the innocent in promise,
While I eternally seek thy in bliss;
My warmth—a winter fireplace,
Thy, its sole burning ember.
An eternal remembrance—my prayer,
Lovingly shan't I reminisce thy in distress,
For thy, my celestial birth-giver.

2. SWEET SWADDLING

As boughs do to chirps,
As tides do to isles,
As wind does to souls alone,
As air does to brown holdings,
As life does to the body,
As hue does to vibrancy,
Thy love swaddles my bijou heart.

3. THE UTOPIAN VISION

Thy sun-like warmth, scorching,
To the soul of the soulless Stygian,
While thy warmth shan't—
It enrapture like sweet serape?
Swaddling under the moon—the sea and tide,
A tie, never to be obliterated; for
In thy radiance, the sun-kissed blush,
While I remain puerile in love.

4. FOR THY I SHALL BE

Frolicking I be at thy sight,
My ephemeral heart
Of my eternal soul,
In this ethereal life.
Fugacious shall be the Stygian,
For thy radiance shall
Lay rooted and entwined
In my love for thee.
For eternity, thy shall—
Bewitch my bijou heart,
While I remain in reverence
To thee, my love!

5. IN THE ABODE OF A CELESTIAL

Heaven's tears shall nourish
From within, while ambrosia
Shall flow in thy name.
Elating my heart to the stars,
While it radiates from within,
My love for thee.
Enamoured is my soul at thy sight,
Embedded is thy radiance, for
Shone art thy in Aphrodite's heart.

6. EPHEMERAL YET ETERNAL

My fervent love shall
Burn as the embers do,
But for eternity, as warmth,
Until thy absence.
Quagmire shall me be invisible,
For thy shall be invincible.
Those turned grey be able,
While thy mellifluous voice shall cradle.
The stoic souls shall turn,
While the Stygian shall burn.
Thy, a sight of an ale,
Yet thy love, for all an ail.

7. AN ETERNAL RYTHM

Suspended roots entwine,
Seeping deep as does my faith,
In thy—our souls shall
Forever osculate in thy radiance,
While stars scintillate timidly.
My soul shall unite with thy,
But not my bijou heart in earth.
Yet for miles, thy lustre
Shall cradle my innocence for thy.
Thy sweet dew-like mind on
Ripened fruit under dawn's light,
Jostling to be held.
Thy effulgence shall bewitch my soul,
While thy absence shall shatter my heart.
Alas, my love, in thy rhythm I dwell eternally.

8. THE PUERILE HEART

To thy ethereal grace,
I shall beseech,
For a soul so radiant
As Venus's sky,
A face so calm yet elated
As a mother's sight on her newborn.
For entwined is my heart
With thy presence, a worldly prayer.
Rooted is thy name
In my diffident love,
For thy, my beacon of hope,
And in moors shan't—
My puerile heart beat eternally.

9. THEN I TURNED

Yearning shall I remain
Beneath the infinite blue sky,
For its showers shall have
My withered soul bloom.
Thy hurricane shall storm my heart,
Wrecking its citadel,
Breaching and leaching off its love,
Only to rebuild it to its glory.

10. HER

Thy spirit, like wild horses,
On wilted grass—wild and free.
Thy curls, like gentle waves,
By cliff sides of the giant blue.
Thy eyes, soft hazel—as shallow
As deep, a graceful gaze.
Thy mellifluous yet firm voice, like
Warmth in dark, treacherous times.
While thy guiding light, since birth,
Shall have thee, mother—
As my puerile heart's want, a soul's decree.

11. HIM

A heart just as fragile in my presence,
As strong to the souls around.
Thy, as eternal ray of warmth radiate,
Forever enigmatic, yet never to me alone.
Thou, a cliff past my vibrant plains,
Never thy let the seas hit in vain.

My soul turned thy purpose,
Painted vibrant my canvas,
Captivated my Stygian when nervous,
For thy, I truly call in reverence—
My Father!

12. PASSION FILLED GAZE

An ethereal gaze to lure,
Unbridled hearts of love,
A sight as though utopian,
Shall have the stern fatuous—
In love; for blinding is thy radiance.
Know shan't thy any boundaries,
Like thy dark eyes—deep and infinite.
And ephemeral art thy anger,
Like a mother to her dear—a spinning
Needle, but of blooms, not needle; pain
Never existent in real, but mist.
Reverberates, doesn't thy love in heart?
Crashing art my thoughts at thy voice,
Forever etched in this enigmatic life.

13. FALLING IN LOVE

A caducous leaf at sixteen,
A sybarite of thy heart,
For thy tinted purse turns
The Stygian's tint to flames.
Ether to stardust, while
Also having my soul and my—
Very heart pervious to thy love.
Thy faint yet bellowing heart,
Rudimentary for love to betide,
Roaring is mine, a battle cry
To win thy love for life,
Like seas of high tide.

14. WHILE IN LOVE

Though thy words shall dissemble,
Thy eyes shan't dear.
Soaring high to the infinite,
Like stardust, thy love; for
Shan't a castle rise of thy radiance,
While I shall be its citadel; thy
My crown jewel, one to revere.
Swaddling my enthralled soul,
While rhythms of thy puerile persiflage lay.
Fallen is my bijou heart for thee,
For now united, it beats.

15. FALLING OUT OF LOVE

Leaves shan't wait to turn till fall,
While buds burn before bloom.
Flowers frolic in dreams alone,
For bees buzz no more.
Shattered, as does glass on fall,
Fed is my heart to the trenches.
My eternal soul, turned ephemeral,
Shan't be revived in the absence of thy.

16. LOVE WORTH REMINISCING

Thy laughter reverberates in time,
Immured and eternal, unlike this
Ephemeral life, art exhilarating,
For thy wants still my necessity.
Thy grace unforgotten, as is thy voice,
Like a father to his heart-like softened rocks.
Thy absence, like high waves on cliffs;
Thy anger, like rumbling thunder over tides,
Steering my vessel while ripping apart
My heart—trashing my now lone soul.
Thy warmth, like an eternal ember, Immured.
Thy love, well reminisced.

17. ASHEN HEART

Thy blades of rage shan't cut
My flesh, nor my then bijou heart;
For it shatters alone, as does ice.
A place warm and serene, now
Runs cold, as Nile turned red.
If not for the eclipse, the moon
Shan't have met the fiery sun,
And I shan't be the dunes of the north—
The lifeless white, utterly disconsolate,
Just as my ashen heart at thy sight.

18. PASSION DEVOID

The sky shall dissemble the sun, for—
Dawn shan't rise at the horizon.
Bees shan't bumble, for the flowers are devoid.
Birds shan't nest, for boughs are devoid.
For shan't the sun rise in the east,
Shan't flowers bloom but turn to weed,
Shan't the moon shine in dread,
For love devoid in life is—
Passion devoid indeed.

19. PASSION FILLED

Lord's heir, mastered art thou,
For thy heaven's mistress,
Blades shall reap no blood,
For turned art into love's martyr.
Thy eyes—dawn's break—shall
Thaw a heart of ages in disdain.
The pyre of worldly hate shan't commence,
For the ashes turned innocent.
Thy strength, like ivory, shall break illusions,
Never to rejoin in vain—thy eternal.

20. RADIANT ART THY

Like winter dew on lotus-tinted,
Like thy faint blush it rests.
Like gravel so fine, in oyster,
In thy, my heart shall gleam.
For thy, the cursed gold—
Worldly treasure yet to be wielded.
And art thy eyes, a sword of ivory,
Piercing deep, thy heavenly radiance blasphemy.
Thy light so radiant,
My soul shall dissolve in thy.

21. HEART'S CONSORT

Net for thy eyes,
Bait for thy talk,
Landed in thy hands,
My delicate, severed heart.
Shan't the sky trade
Its timid twilight
For thy tinted cheek;
The peony's disguise?
Thy passion shall rid
The moon of its chasms,
Flooding them full—
Shall they turn to blossoms,
For thy my heart's consort.

www.ingramcontent.com/pod-product-compliance
Lightning Source LLC
La Vergne TN
LVHW021719210726
843509LV00021B/2893